RECORDS OF THE AYRSHIRE MILITIA

FROM 1802 TO 1883

(PRIVATELY PRINTED 1884)

© 2011 South Ayrshire Libraries

Inrodution

by

Tom Barclay, Local Studies Librarian,

South Ayrshire Council

Typesetting by JimandZetta.com

This slim volume, privately printed in 1884, was based on hand-written records in a note-book kept in Ayr Barracks. It consists of a year-by-year account of the activities of the Ayrshire Militia from the time of its formation in 1802, along with tables showing the regimental strength at different periods, and some lists of officers. In particular it chronicles the regiment's Napoleonic War service in Scotland, England and Ireland from 1803 until 1816, using contemporary journal entries.

During the Revolutionary and Napoleonic Wars with France, which lasted almost continuously from 1793 until 1815, the British regular army found itself stretched to the limit at home and abroad. To assist in guarding against invasion and maintaining internal security a variety of auxiliary home-defence units were raised. There were many volunteer units of varying quality, but the militia – raised by selective conscription – constituted a better-organised national reserve force. In the late nineteenth century (by which time militia service had become voluntary) Ayrshire's militia became part of the Royal Scots Fusiliers, and it maintained a distinct identity within that regiment until 1919.

The 'H. H. D.' who edited the manuscript records and had them privately printed in 1884 was the Honourable Hew Hamilton-Dalrymple (1857-1945, knighted 1932), third son of the 10th Earl of Stair. He was at the time a captain in what was then the 4th Battalion, Royal Scots Fusiliers, and which a few years later became the 3rd (Militia) Battalion RSF. He was promoted to major, and retired with the honorary rank of Lieutenant-Colonel of the battalion.

A new introduction, written by Tom Barclay – Local Studies Librarian, South Ayrhsire Libraries - providing additional information has been added by the library service.

South Ayrshire Libraries acknowledge the help and assistance provided by Jim and Zetta Brown of JimandZetta.com in producing this reprinted version.

Introduction

This slim volume, privately printed in 1884, was based on hand-written records in a note-book kept in Ayr Barracks. It consists of a year-by-year account of the activities of the Ayrshire Militia from the time of its formation in 1802, along with tables showing the regimental strength at different periods, and some lists of officers. In particular it chronicles the regiment's Napoleonic War service in Scotland, England and Ireland from 1803 until 1816, using contemporary journal entries.

During the Revolutionary and Napoleonic Wars with France, which lasted almost continuously from 1793 until 1815, the British regular army found itself stretched to the limit at home and abroad. To assist in guarding against invasion and maintaining internal security a variety of auxiliary home-defence units were raised. The formation of corps of volunteers was encouraged, and these included the Ayrshire Yeomanry Cavalry, the

Ayrshire Volunteers (infantry armed with smooth-bore muskets) and the Ayrshire Rifle Volunteers. Volunteer units provided their own equipment, and so generally consisted of the wealthier members of society. They could not be compelled to serve outside their local area, chose their own officers, and were responsible for their own training and discipline – the military effectiveness of volunteers was frequently questioned. The militia, raised by selective conscription and equipped by the government, was a separate force which had a much greater degree of organisation, uniformity, and flexibility. Its regiments were intended as reinforcements for the regular army – capable if necessary of standing in the line of battle – whereas volunteers were only expected to engage in harassment and guerrilla warfare. More efficient volunteer units designated local militia were created in 1808 – the old volunteer units were abolished in 1813 – and the militia proper was then referred to as the regular militia.

In England a properly-organised

militia had existed since 1757, but north of the border it was brought into being by the Scottish Militia Acts of 1797 and 1802. In each parish, a list (updated annually) of all able-bodied men of military age had to be compiled by the schoolmasters or burgh constables. When a ballot for militia service was to be held, the county lieutenancy court (presided over by the Lord Lieutenant) arranged for these parish lists to be gathered together, and the names on them written down on folded pieces of paper. Names were then drawn at random until the full quota set for the county militia regiment had been made up. Service (usually for five years) was compulsory for those whose names had been drawn, unless; they were in an exempt category (including apprentices, seafarers, clergy, and poor men who were fathers of two or more young children); they could arrange for a substitute; or they could pay a substantial penalty. As the better-off could use the latter two alternatives to evade service, the militia, in contrast to the volunteers, tended to consist of the poorer classes – the enlistment bounty and active-service pay induced many needy individuals to offer themselves as substitutes. Militia regiments were equipped and trained similarly to the regular army's line infantry regiments. Militiamen were subject to the harsh discipline of the regular army, and although they could not be compelled to serve overseas, their unit could be sent anywhere within Britain and Ireland. A bounty was paid to militiamen who volunteered to transfer to the regular army. Many whose names were drawn for militia service absconded before they could be formally enrolled, and many others deserted from the ranks. Supplementary ballots were necessary from time to time to keep militia units up to strength.

The 7th North British Militia (Ayr and Renfrew) had been raised as a result of the 1797 Scottish Militia Act, and stood down following the Peace of Amiens in 1802. Non-commissioned officers and drummers from that unit then formed the core of the Ayrshire Militia, created under the provisions of the 1802 Scottish Militia Act. Its headquarters was in the county town of Ayr, where a former sugar refinery near the harbour had been converted into a barracks in 1794. The regiment was mobilised ('embodied') for active service in 1803 (war re-commenced during the year) and served continuously from then until disembodied at Ayr in 1816. (The volunteer local militia was disbanded in that year, but the yeomanry cavalry remained active to counter Radical unrest.) In each of the years 1820, 1821 and 1829, the regiment – which in 1813 had been granted the title of The Prince Regent's Royal Regiment of Ayrshire Militia – was assembled for a few weeks' training. However, ballots had been discontinued after 1825, and the strength was eventually reduced to a very small permanent staff.

The militia throughout Britain was embodied for home service during the 1854-56 war with Russia ('The Crimean War'). The title of the Ayrshire Militia was changed to The Prince Regent's Royal Regiment of Ayrshire Rifles, or Royal Ayrshire Rifles. There was no resort to balloting, the ranks being filled by volunteers. From 1858 on, there were annual training assemblies. The threat of war with France in 1859 saw the formation of the Scottish Volunteer Force. Corps of rifle volunteers were formed throughout the country, including the 1st Battalion, Ayrshire Rifle Volunteers (joined by a second battalion in 1873). The volunteers and militia were separately organised, but as militia service was now voluntary, and as they could both be popularly referred to as 'Ayrshire Rifles', the distinction between them became blurred. This resulted in title changes for the militia, which became the Royal Ayrshire Regiment of Militia Rifles in 1860 and The Prince Regent's Royal Regiment of Ayr and Wigtown Militia in 1866 – the two Wigtownshire companies of the Galloway Rifles (militia) had been incorporated in 1860.

The army reforms of 1881 allotted each regular army regiment a specific area in which it was based and from which it recruited, and attached to it the militia units of that area. The

Royal Scots Fusiliers, with its depot at Ayr Barracks, was allocated Ayrshire and the Scottish border counties. To its two regular battalions were added the Scottish Borderers (Dumfries) Militia, which became its 3rd Battalion, and the Royal Ayr and Wigtown Militia, which became its 4th Battalion. In 1887 the 3rd Battalion was transferred to the King's Own Scottish Borderers, and the 4th Battalion was renumbered as the 3rd (Militia) Battalion Royal Scots Fusiliers. As part of the 1908 army reforms the militia was renamed the special reserve, and the unit was re-designated the 3rd (Special Reserve) Battalion RSF. On the outbreak of the First World War in 1914 it was embodied, being engaged throughout the war in the training of recruits for service in the RSF's active-service battalions. In 1919, following the end of the war, the battalion was disbanded. This finally brought to an end the story of the unit which had been formed in 1802 to face Napoleon's invasion threat, with continuity from the 7th North British Militia of 1797. (In 1887 the two battalions of Ayrshire Rifle Volunteers raised in 1860 and 1873 became the 1st and 2nd Volunteer Battalions of the Royal Scots Fusiliers, and when the Territorial Army was formed in 1908 they became the regiment's 4th and 5th (T.A.) Battalions.)

The 'H. H. D.' who edited the manuscript records and had them privately printed in 1884 was the Honourable Hew Hamilton-Dalrymple (1857-1945, knighted 1932), third son of the 10th Earl of Stair. He was at the time a captain in what was then the 4th Battalion, Royal Scots Fusiliers, and which a few years later became the 3rd (Militia) Battalion RSF. He was promoted to major, and retired with the honorary rank of Lieutenant-Colonel of the battalion.

Summary of changes of title and uniform

1802 – The Ayrshire Militia
(Numbered the 38th regiment of militia, but this was seldom used)
Uniform red with buff facings (collar and cuffs)

1813 – The Prince Regent's Royal Regiment of Ayrshire Militia
Uniform red with blue facings – first issued Christmas Day 1813

1854 – The Prince Regent's Royal Regiment of Ayrshire Rifles (Royal Ayrshire Rifles)
(Now numbered the 115th regiment of militia)
Uniform green with scarlet facings

1860 – The Royal Ayrshire Regiment of Militia Rifles
Uniform as before, thistle badge

1866 – The Prince Regent's Royal Regiment of Ayr and Wigtown Militia

Uniform red with blue facings

1881 – 4th Battalion (Royal Ayr and Wigtown Militia) Royal Scots Fusiliers
Uniform from this time on – that of the RSF

1887 – 3rd Battalion (Royal Ayr and Wigtown Militia) Royal Scots Fusiliers

1908-1919 – 3rd Battalion (Special Reserve) Royal Scots Fusiliers

Militia uniforms were generally similar to the regular army issue for the line infantry. During 1854 – 1866, the uniform would have been similar to that of the green-jacketed regular rifle regiments.

Colours

1803 – 1868 In Ayr Auld Kirk

1868 – 1889 In Lochinch Castle near Stranraer, the seat of the earls of Stair

1889 – 1919 In the Royal Scots Fusiliers bay, Scottish War Memorial, Edinburgh Castle

The 1797-1802 colours of the 7th North British Militia (Ayr and Renfrew) were laid up in Paisley Abbey.

Records of the Ayrshire Militia From 1802 to 1883

(Privately printed in 1884)
Published by South Aysrhire Libraries
© 2011
ISBN: 978 0901567 277
Typestting by jimandzetta.com

NOTE.

It has been my object in having these records printed to preserve them, as they are at present merely in manuscript in a small Book in the Militia Orderly Room at Ayr Barracks; and also in hope that they may interest past and present members of the Regiment.

It was my intention, when I first thought of having them printed, to include, if possible, some records of the Galloway Militia, as two Companies of that Regiment were incorporated in the Ayr Militia on the breaking up of the former, but I have been unable to find any records of it.

I have occasionally altered the

original wording, omitting what I thought unnecessary, and adding a few notes of my own.

H. H. D.

May 14th, 1884

RECORDS OF THE AYRSHIRE MILITIA.

The original formation of the Ayrshire Militia was made in the year 1802, from the disembodied non-commissioned officers of the then Ayr and Renfrew of 7th North British Militia, commanded by the Earl of Glasgow. The non-commissioned officers and drummers who were told off to form the Ayrshire Militia were placed under the command of Col. Lord Montgomerie, whose commission as Colonel was dated October 22d, 1802. The regiment was ordered to be stationed in the county town of Ayrshire. On November 29th of the same year, a ballot took place for 436 men, that being the establishment fixed by the Act (42d George III). The men were enrolled on the 3d, 13th, and 22d December of the same year, under the superintendence of the Colonel, Lord Montgomerie, and the Adjutant, George Clarke. The following was the fixed establishment: –

	Colonel.	Lt.-Colonel.	Major.	Captains.	Lieutenants.	Ensigns.	Adjutant.	Quarter-Master.	Surgeon.	Sergeant-Major.	Qr.-Master Sergt.	Sergeants.	Corporals.	Drummers.	Privates.
Total,	1	1	1	7	8	6	1	1	1	1	1	21	21	15	436

During this year orders were issued from Whitehall and the War Office, arranging the manner of paying and clothing the disembodied Militia. A meeting also of the Lieutenancy and Field Officers (viz. Earl of Eglinton,

Lord Lieutenant, and Col. Lord Montgomerie, Lt.-Colonel Sir Hew Dalrymple Hamilton, and the Adjutant) took place, at which it was resolved that the facings of the regiment should be buff[1] and the number of companies of the Battalion 7, including one of Grenadiers. The officers were nominated at this meeting by the Lord Lieutenant of the county. The following is a list of the Officers nominated:—

Col., Lord Montgomerie.[2]

Lt.-Colonel, Sir Hew Dalrymple

---

[1] In the original the wording is as follows:— The facings were fixed on to be light orange or dark yellow, or rather betwixt these two colours.

[2] Archibald, Lord Montgomerie (1773-1814) was born at Bourtreehill on the 30th July 1773. He served first as Ensign in 42d Foot. He was appointed Colonel of Ayrshire Militia, October 22d, 1802. He resigned his commission 1807. In 1809 he became Major-General, and he was employed on active service in Sicily in 1812-1813. He died at Alicant 1814 (4th January), and was buried in the Convent Chapel at Gibraltar.

Hamilton, Bart.

Major, James Fergusson.

Captain, Sir D. H. Blair, Bart.

Captain, William Crawford

Captain, John Hamilton.

Captain, James H. Blair.

Captain, John Taylor.

Captain, James F. Gray.

Captain, Charles S. McAlester.

Lieutenant, William Duncan.

Lieutenant, James Young.

Lieutenant, William A. Smith.

Lieutenant, William Pagan.

Lieutenant, Duncan McIntyre.

Lieutenant, Andrew Campbell.

Ensign, M. D. Fergushill.

Ensign, John A Bell.

Ensign, Patrick Auld.

Ensign, Andrew Hair.

Ensign, Alexander F. Gray.
Ensign, David Johnston.
Adjutant, George Clarke.
Quarter-Master, John Bell.
Surgeon, William Donaldson.

In the beginning of 1803 the King's warrant was signed, calling out the Militia for active service, on account of the disturbances in France, and the Lord Lieutenant ordered the officers of the Ayrshire Militia to assemble on the 4th of April, and the men on the 6th.

April 6

There appeared to be the following numbers, which were enrolled or balloted into companies as per annexed state:—

STATE OF THE REGIMENT 6TH APRIL

1803

Officers present.							Non-commissioned Officers.		Rank and file.				Wanting.		
Colonel.	Lt.-Colonel.	Major.	Captains.	Lieutenants.	Ensigns.	Staff.	Sergeants.	Drummers.	Present and fit for duty.	Sick.	On Furlough.	Total.	Sergeants.	Drummers.	Rank and File.
...	...	...	6	5	4	3	19	7	383	2	2	387	3	8	70

1803

The absentees were balloted for according to the Act, and enrolments took place almost daily.

May 4

The arms and accoutrements were issued to the regiment.

June 15

The colours were presented to the Regiment by Lady Montgomerie.

The only duty of the regiment while it remained at Ayr was the ordinary barrack guard.

June 18

Marched in three divisions for Dundee barracks and town.

June 27

Arrived at Dundee barracks.

June 30

A supplementary militia of 218 men were called out, and the establishment consequently changed to 1 colonel, 1 lieutenent-colonel, 1 major, 8 captains,

10 lieutenents, 6 ensigns, 3 staff, 1 sergeant-major, 1 quarter-master sergeant, 30 sergeants, 18 drummers, and 686 rank and file—the numbers continuing to be filled up according to law.

August 14

Five companies march to Kirkcaldy headquarters, and three to Perth, where they arrive the same day.

October 25

The regiment march from its quarters at Kirkcaldy and Perth for Dalkeith, where the division from Kirkcaldy arrives same day.

October 27

    The division from Perth arrive at Dalkeith.

October 28

    The regiment march for Dunbar barracks.

October 29

    Arrive at Dunbar barracks, and placed in Major-General Don's brigade.

November 11

    The first half-yearly inspection made by Major-General Don. Major-General Don has great pleasure in acquainting the brigade, which was seen yesterday by General and Earl of Moira, that his lordship was highly pleased with their appearance and steadiness under arms.

November 17

Reviewed by the Earl of Moira, commander of the forces. The duties of the regiment here consisted of the barrack guards and the town and fort guards of Dunbar.

December 30

March for Edinburgh Castle.

1804

January 3

Arrive at Edinburgh Castle, and placed in Brigadier-General the Earl of Dalhousie's brigade.

January 4

Orders received to form the regiment into 10 companies, per War Office letter, dated 22d December 1803.

May 11

The half-yearly inspection made by Brigadier-General the Earl of Dalhousie.

September 4

The half-yearly inspection made by Brigadier-General the Earl of Dalhousie. The duties of the regiment, while it lay in Edinburgh Castle, were its share of the castle and city guards, with detachments over the French prisoners of war at Greenlaw.

1805

February 27

March from Edinburgh Castle for Newcastle-upon-Tyne.

Arrive at Newcastle, and placed in Major-General the Honourable George Gray's Brigade.

April 2

The half-yearly inspection made by Major-General Gray.

April 16

Received an order to permit volunteering to the line, dated 13th April 1805, in consequence of which, 1 officer and 77 men extend their services.

May 27

    Reviewed by Lieutenant-General Sir Hew Dalrymple, commanding the Northern District.

June 3

    March in two divisions for Colchester barracks.

June 26

    After a pleasant march, the regiment arrive at Colchester barracks.

June 27

    Inspected by Major-General Sir David Baird, and placed in Major-General Sherbrook's brigade.

July 16

Brigadier-General Lord Montgomerie appointed to the command of the brigade, of which the regiment formed a part. The establishment reduced to 7 companies and 436 privates.

September 11

The half-yearly inspection made by Brigadier General Lord Montgomerie.

October 17

Reviewed by His Royal Highness the Duke of York on Boxted Heath.

November 28

Marched to Weeley barracks, and placed in Brigadier-General Lord

Montgomerie's brigade.

1806

May 1

The half-yearly inspection made by Brigadier-General Lord Montgomerie. The duties of the regiment at this station and at Colchester consisted of the ordinary garrison guards, and detachments through the county of Essex over magazines, signal-posts, etc., etc.

May 28

March for Maldon.

May 29

Arrive at Maldon.

June 16

March for Chelmsford and Danbury, and placed in Major-General Murray's brigade.

September 6

The half-yearly inspection made by Major-General Murray.

September 23

Reviewed by Lieutenant-General the Earl of Chatham at Danbury.

1807

March 12

The half-yearly inspection made by Major-General Murray. The chief duties at this station were the ordinary garrison guards, and detachments for the arsenal at Purfleet.

June 26

March from Chelmsford for Portsmouth.

July 2

Arrive at Portsmouth, and stationed in Portsea barracks, Major-General Sir George Prevost commanding.

July 4

Reviewed on Southsea Common by Major-General Sir George Prevost.

August 17

Encamp on Southsea Common.

August 21

An order received to permit a certain proportion of the militia to volunteer to the line, dated 15th August. In consequence of which, 4 officers and 216 men extend their services, which reduced the effectives to 313, but the establishment remained the same.

September 15

The half-yearly inspection made by Major-General Sir George Prevost.

October 1

The tents struck, and marched into Portsea barracks.

October 6

Marched from Portsea barracks to Four House barracks, Portsmouth.

October 16

Lieutenant-Colonel Sir D. Hunter Blair, Captain D. S. Buchanan, the adjutant, 4 sergeants, 6 corporals, 2 drummers, and 30 privates proceed to Ayr for the purpose of receiving a levy of 327 men about to be balloted.

October 25

Sir D. Hunter Blair appointed colonel in consequence of the resignation of Lord Montgomerie. The duties of the regiment, while it lay at Portsmouth, consisted in the garrison and dockyard guards.

November 7

Marched from Portsmouth to Gosport, placed in Brigadier-General Porter's brigade, and stationed in the New Military Hospital barracks.

November 25

The establishment of the regiment increased (*vide* War Office letter, 28th November 1807), as per annexed detail.

INCREASED ESTABLISHMENT

Colonel.	Lieut.-Colonel.	Major.	Captains.	Lieutenants.	Ensigns.	Adjutant.	Quarter-Master.	Surgeon.	Sergeant-Major.	Qr.-Mast. Sergt.	Sergeants.	Corporals.	Drum-Major.	Drummers.	Privates.	Total.
1	1	1	7	8	6	1	1	1	1	1	29	29	1	15	599	702

1808

February 8

Levy from the county join, consisting of 275 men.

February 22

Marched to Gosport old barracks.

April 20

The half-yearly inspection made by Brigadier-General Porter

August 10

Volunteer unanimously to serve in Spain. The chief duty at this station was over the French prisoners of war within the garrison prison, and on board prison ships in the Lake of Porchester.

October 10

    March from Gosport for the Sussex District.

October 13

    Arrive at Horsham barracks, Colonel Wood of the East Middlesex Militia, commanding. The only duties here are the ordinary guards of the garrison.

1809

February 1

    March for Silverhill barracks.

February 3

    Arrive at Silverhill barracks.

March 24

An order received to permit volunteering to the line, to commence on the 1st of April, by which 3 officers and 152 men extend their service, and agreeable to the Act, the deficiency to be filled up by beat of drum.

May 29

The half-yearly inspection made by Brigadier-General Baron Alten.

May 31

A party, under the command of Captain Chalmers, proceed to Ayrshire on recruiting service. The chief duties here have been the ordinary guards of the garrison.

June 19

    March for Eastburn barracks.

June 20

    Arrive at Eastburn, and placed in Major-General the Earl of Dalhousie's brigade. The duties here were barrack guards, and Martello Towers.

July 5

    March to Blachington barracks. Chief duties, detachments on the coast and barrack guards.

August 9

    March for Portsmouth.

August 12

    Arrive at Portsmouth, and embark

on board three transports for Leith.

August 14

Drop down to Spithead.

August 22

Sail under convoy of the Dextrous Gun-Brig, Captain Tomlinson.

August 29

Arrive in Leith harbour.

August 3o

Disembark and march to Prestonpans.

September 2

Inspected by Major-General Leslie, under whose command the regiment is placed.

September 4

March into Musselburgh barracks.

November 8

The half-yearly inspection made by Major-General Leslie. The duties here consist of detachments to Pennycuick, and the ordinary garrison guards.

1810

April 30

The regiment march in two divisions for Ayr barracks and town.

May 5

Arrive at Ayr. Detachments sent

from this station to Ballantrae and Portpatrick.

June 2

The half-yearly inspection made by Major-General Lord Elphinstone.

July 6

A detachment, consisting of one sergeant, one corporal, and nineteen privates, under the command of Lieutenant Philips, embark for the island of Arran. A ballot takes place, whereby the establishment is nearly completed.

October 23

The half-yearly inspection made by Major-General Lord Elphinstone.

1811

May 4

An order received to permit volunteering to the line on the 10th instant.

May 10

The quota of volunteers (one officer and sixty-two men) turn out and are attested.

May 11

The volunteers march to Hamilton under the command of Captain Stevenson. Continue successfully to fill up the vacancies by beat of drum.

June 12

The half-yearly inspection made by

Major-General Peter.

July 9

An order received, dated Whitehall, 5th July 1811, to permit the interchange of the British and Irish militia.

August 5

The officers, non-commissioned officers, and privates (one corporal and thirty privates accepted), have extended their services, and have been enrolled for the militia of the United Kingdom.

September 2

A detachment, consisting of two companies, under the command of

Captain Stevenson, march for Greenock and Port Glasgow, and another one of company, under the command of Lieutenant Campbell, march for Dumfries.

September 25

The establishment reduced to the original quota fixed by the Act.

November 22

The half-yearly inspection made by Major-General Thomas Peter. The chief duties at this station have consisted of the detachments mentioned, and the usual town and barrack guards.

1812

February 14

Colonel William Kelso appointed colonel of the regiment, *vice* Sir David Hunter Blair, resigned.

March 5

The regiment march for Paisley. The out parties, except those at Greenock and Port-Glasgow, called in.

March 6

Arrive at Paisley.

March 9

The detachment at Greenock and Port-Glasgow form the garrison of Dumbarton, under the command of Captain Stevenson. A detachment of one company, under the command of Lieutenant Fletcher, march to Greenock.

April 29

An order received for the volunteering of the annual quota to the line, to commence on 4th May next.

May 4

Volunteering commences.

May 9

The quota of volunteers, 1 officer and 62 privates, completed, and march for their respective destinations under the command of Lieutenant McKie.

May 25

Recruiting parties, under the command of Lieutenant-Colonel Farquhar, march to the country for the purpose of recruiting supernumeraries by beat of drum.

June 27

The half-yearly inspection made by Major-General Durham commanding the district. The chief duty here is the detachment at Dumbarton Castle over General Simon and several other French prisoners of war.

July 27

March for Edinburgh.

July 30

Arrive at Edinburgh, stationed in Queensberry House barracks, and placed in the Major-General Scott's brigade.

November 6

The half-yearly inspection made by Lieutenant-General Wynyard commanding the forces.

1813

January 4

The clothing of the regiment inspected by Major-General Thomas Scott.

February 4

The regiment fire a *feu-de-joie*, in honour of Her Majesty's birthday, on the Castle Hill.

February 25

In consequence of the regiment expressing its abhorrence of the conduct of several men in some of the regiments of Scotch militia, and disclaiming any knowledge of or participation in their proceedings, it receives the approbation of the Commander of the Forces in General Orders (*vide* General Order, dated Adjutant-General's Office, Edinburgh, 25th February 1813), and that of Major-General Scott, commanding the brigade (*vide* Brigade Order of 26th February

1813). The thanks of the Lord Lieutenant of the county of Ayr (*vide* his letter dated Irvine, 10th of March 1813), and the approbation of the Commander-in-Chief, of the uniform zeal and good conduct of the regiment (*vide* Adjutant-General's Letters, dated Horse Guards, 16th March 1813).

April 1

Volunteering to the line commences, when 47 men offer their services, and are attested.

April 2

The number of volunteers completed, more than the quota having offered.

April 24

The Lord Lieutenant of the county of Ayr notifies to Colonel Kelso that His Royal Highness the Prince Regent is pleased to approve of the Ayrshire Militia being styled His Royal Highness the Prince Regent's Royal Regiment of Ayrshire Militia, and to have blue facings.

May 27

The half-yearly inspection made by Major-General Thomas Scott on Bruntsfield Links.

June 4

The regiment fire a *feu-de-joie*, in honour of His Majesty's birthday, on Bruntsfield Links.

June 12

Communicated from the Horse Guards that His Royal Highness the Prince Regent has been pleased, in the name and on the behalf of His Majesty, to approve of the Ayrshire Militia being in future styled, "The Prince Regent's Royal Regiment of Ayrshire Militia."

July 9

The regiment march in two divisions, by Queensferry and Kinross, for Perth.

July 13

Arrive at Perth, and placed in Major-General Graham's brigade. Chief duty at the depot over prisoners of war.

July 16

A great proportion of the regiment quartered in town. The Wilts, Durham, and Royal Ayr compose the brigade.

An order received from the Secretary of State to increase the supernumeraries, to be raised by beat of drum, to one-half the number of private men borne on the establishment, and to recruit at the head-quarters of the regiment, and any place within ten miles thereof.

October 26

The half-yearly inspection made by Major-General Samuel Graham on the

North Inch of Perth.

November 28

An Act of Parliament and Instructions, dated Whitehall, 25th November 1813, received, permitting volunteering either to the line or as European militia, not exceeding three-fourths of the number actually serving in the regiment.

December 25

The clothing for the year 1814 fitted, and inspected by Major-General Graham. Facings *blue*.

1814

January 1

The volunteering terminates, Captain Patrick, Ensign Ralston, and 71 men, having turned out, been approved, and attested for the line. None of the men have offered to extend their services as militia, notwithstanding almost the whole of the officers having offered to accompany them to any part of Europe.

February 3

An order received, dated Horse Guards, 26th January 1814, for the regiment to be inspected, preparatory to its being sent to Ireland.

February 4

The regiment inspected accordingly by Major-General Graham.

February 12

A route received for the march of the regiment, in three divisions, on the 14th, 15th, and 16th instant, for Ayr town.

February 24

The last division arrived in Ayr, and billeted in the town.

February 26

A route received for the march of the regiment, in three divisions, on the 4th, 5th, and 7th of March next for Port Patrick, there to embark for Donaghadee.

March 9

The first division arrive at

Donaghadee, and receive orders to proceed to Belfast by divisions on their landing at Donaghadee.

March 13

The last division arrive in Belfast, and a route received for the march of the regiment, in two divisions, on the 14th and 15th instant, to Auchnacloy, in the county Tyrone.

March 17

The first division arrive at Auchnacloy, and quartered in town.

March 18

The second division arrive, and the whole marched into barracks, Major-General Coghlan, at Armagh, commanding the brigade.

March 19

Captain Buttle and Moncrieff's companies detached to Omagh, agreeable to route, under the command of Captain Buttle.

April 4

The annual volunteering to the line takes place, when only 7 men extend their services, and are attested.

May 10

The detachment at Omagh inspected by Major-General Burnet.

May 19

The half-yearly inspection made at

Auchnacloy by Major-General Coghlan, on which occasion the general was pleased to express his entire approbation of the appearance and discipline of the corps; *vide* brigade orders of this date.

June 12

Routes received for the march of the regiment from its present quarters at Auchnacloy and Omagh to Cavan, on the 13th, 14th, and 20th instant.

June 16

The first division arrived at Cavan, and detached 1 sergeant and 21 rank and file to Bailleboro, under the command of Lieutenant Alexander.

June 19

The second division arrive at Caravan. Captain Adlam's company detached to Virginia, 1 sergeant and 30 rank and file to Killnaluck, under Lieutenant Campbell, and 1 sergeant and 30 rank and file to Ardee, under Ensign McVittie.

June 22

The last division arrived at Cavan, and the whole accommodated in barracks. The only duties at Cavan, a small barrack guard, with a guard on the county gaol, and the suppression of illicit distillation in the neighbourhood. The duties of the detachments are the suppression of smuggling and keeping the peace.

July 31

Detachments march from headquarters as follows:—

1 sergeant and 30 rank and file to Stradene, under Lieutenant Phillips

Do. do. to Ballyhaise, under Lieutenant Bebram.

Do. do. to Bally, under Ensign McKean.

August 27

1 sergeant and 30 rank and file detached to Cootehill, under the command of Ensign Kerr.

Since the regiment's arrival in this quarter it has been under the command of Major-General Prince Kimmer and Honourable Stephen Mahon, who successively commanded at Enniskillen.

October 12

The half-yearly inspection made by Major-General the Honourable Stephen Mahon, on which occasion the general was highly satisfied with every department of the regiment; *vide* brigade orders of 13th October 1814.

December 3

Captain Adlam's company at Virginia detached 1 sergeant and 18 rank and file to Mount Connaught, under the command of Ensign Gemmell, on account of several disturbances in that neighbourhood.

December 26

Captain Adlam having obtained leave of absence, on account of ill-health, Captain Campbell proceeds to Virginia to command the detachment stationed there and at Mount Connaught.

1815

April 18

An order received from the Secretary of State for Home Department, dated Whitehall, 14th April 1815, to discharge all the men who had completed their term of five years' service, at the following periods, viz,

    One-fourth on the 10th of May next,
    One-fourth on the 10th of June next,
    One-fourth on the 10th of July next,
    And one-fourth on the 10th of

August next, commencing with those hwo have been longest in service.

May 9

The half-yearly inspection made by Major-General Burnet.

May 10

First quota, consisting of 64 men, discharged, agreeable to Secretary of State's orders.

June 10

Second quota discharged, consisting of 64 privates.

July 10

Third quota discharged, consisting of 64 privates.

August 10

Last quota discharged, consisting of 68 privates.

The regiment only remains 118 privates.

August 17

The regiment march from Cavan to Auchnacloy barracks, agreeable to route.

August 19

Arrive at Auchnacloy, and placed under the command of Lieutenant-General Hart at Armagh. No very particular duty at this station.

September 25

New clothing for the present year

issued.

October 10

Marched back to Omagh barracks, and placed in the Londonderry brigade, under the command of Major-General Burnet.

October 12

The autumnal half-yearly inspection made by Major-General Burnet.

1816

January 23

The regiment march from Omagh for Belfast by way of Dungannon.

January 26

    The regiment marched into Belfast from Lisburne.

March 1

    The regiment march from Belfast to Donaghadee *en route* for Scotland; arrive in Portpatrick 2d March.

March 4

    March from Portpatrick to Stranraer.

March 9

    March from Stranraer to Ballantrae.

March 11

    March from Ballantrae to Girvan.

March 12

   March from Girvan to Ayr.

March 23

   The regiment was disembodied; kept on staff 1 adjutant, 1 quarter-master, sergeant-major 1, sergeants 14, corporals 15, drummers 8.

   During the period the regiment was embodied since 1803, although the strength was only 436 men, it gave 11 officers and 694 men as volunteers to the line.

1819

April 12

   Staff reduced to 1 sergeant-major, 11 sergeants, 10 corporals and 4 drummers.

1820

June 26

The regiment assembled for twenty-eight days' training; were in billets and received rations.

1821

July 5

Regiment assembled for twenty-one days' training; were in billets and received rations.

1829

June 15

Regiment assembled for twenty-eight days' training; were in billets and drew rations.

1836
June 25

Permanent staff reduced to 1 adjutant, 1 sergeant-major, 10 sergeants, 4 drummers (no vacancies) having been filled up, as the staff became non-effective.

1846
February 3

Mr. Miller, late Scots Fusilier Guards, appointed Adjutant. The staff at this date consisted of 1 sergeant-major only, and no men on the strength of the regiment, the ballot having been suspended since 1825.

June 4

Earl of Eglinton appointed Colonel-Commandant of the regiment, *vice* Kelso, deceased.

June 8

The strength of the permanent staff was increased to—

1 adjutant, 1 sergeant-major, 5 sergeants.

1852

April 8

Colonel the Honourable F. McAdam

Cathcart succeeds the Earl of Eglinton as Colonel-Commandant of the regiment.

1854

October 26

First commenced enrolling volunteers, in terms of the Act 17 and 18 Vic. cap. 106.

October 30

The title of the regiment to continue the same as before, with the exception of the word "Rifles," which is to be substituted for "Militia."

The regiment will therefore be styled, "The Prince Regent's Royal Regiment of Ayrshire Rifles."

Short title, "Royal Ayrshire Rifles."

The quota and establishment of the regiment was fixed at—

Colonel	Lieutenant-Colonel.	Major.	Captains.	Lieutenants.	Ensigns.	Adjutant.	Quarter-Master.	Surgeon.	Pay-Master.	Sergeant-Major.	Sergeants.	Corporals.	Drum-Major.	Bugles.	Privates.
1	1	1	8	8	8	1	1	1	1	1	24	24	...	8	691

War Office – Sept. 21, 1854, and 17, and 18 Vic. cap. 106, and 17 and 18 Vic. cap. 109.

The ballot was suspended, and the quota was to be raised by voluntary enlistment.

1855

May 1

Colonel the Honourable F. McAdam

Cathcart retires as Honorary Colonel, and is succeeded by Sir Thomas Montgomerie Cunningham as Lieutenant-Colonel Commandant.

The regiment was embodied and quartered in Ayr Barracks.

The regiment was disembodied at the close of the Crimean war, on the 10th of July 1856, and the permanent staff consisted of—

Adjutant.	Quarter-Master.	Sergeant-Major.	Quarter-Master Sergeant.	Pay-Master Sergeant.	Sergeants.	Buglers.
1	1	1	1	1	16	8

1857

The regiment was not called out for training, but each volunteer received

£1, 1s. training bounty.

1858

Sir T. M. Cunninghame, Bart., retires, and is succeeded by Sir James Fergusson, Bart., of Kilkerran, as Lieutenant-Colonel Commandant.

October 5

The regiment assembled for twenty-one days' training. Men were quartered in Ayr Barracks and in billets.

In consequence of wet weather an additional seven days' training was authorized. The men received rations at the Government price, viz. 4½d.

1859

June 30

The regiment assembled for twenty-one days' training, and were quartered in billets, and received rations at the Government price, 4½d.

September 17

The permanent staff of the regiment was increased to the following strength, viz—

Adjutant.	Quarter-Master.	Sergeant-Major.	Quarter-Master Sergeant.	Pay-Master Sergeant.	Orderly Room Clerk.	Hospital Sergeant.	Bugle Major.	Sergeant I. of M.	Sergeants.	Buglers.	
1	1	1	1	1	1	1	1	1 Add.	16 4	8 2	for Wigtown quota.

1860

May 1

The Wigtownshire quota of the Galloway Rifles were amalgamated with the Royal Ayrshire Rifles, the establishment of which is—2 captains, 2 lieutenants, 2 ensigns, 5 sergeants, 5 corporals, 2 buglers, 150 privates. And 4 sergeants and 2 buglers are added to the permanent staff.

June 1

The regiment assembled for twenty-seven days' training, and were quartered in billets, and received rations at the Government price—4½d. for 1 lb. bread ¾ lb. of meat.

War Office, Pall Mall, August 15, 1860

The title of the regiment altered to

ROYAL AYRSHIRE REGIMENT OF MILITIA RIFLES.

Distinctive badge—Thistle.

Approved by Her Majesty.

(Signed) S. HERBERT.

1861

May 1

The regiment assembled for twenty-one days' training, and were quartered in billets, and received rations at the government price, 4½d. for 1 lb. bread ¾ lb. meat.

1862

June 4

Ditto.

1864

May 3

The regiment assembled for twenty-one days' training. About 319 men were quartered in billets, the remainder in barracks. Received rations at the Government price, 4½d. for 1 lb. bread ¾ lb. meat.

August 23

    Strength of regiment reduced to
    10 volunteer sergeants.
    30 corporals.
    600 privates.

W. O. Circular, dated
Aug. 23, 1864.

A.

MILITIA.

821.

1865

June 19

The regiment assembled for twenty-seven day's training, and encamped on the Racecourse, Ayr.

1866

July 9

Ditto.

War Office, Dec. 7, 1866. A. Ayr. 300.

Her Majesty has been graciously pleased to approve of the designation of the regiment being changed to "The Prince Regent's Royal Regiment of Ayr and Wigtown Militia," and of the uniform being red with blue facings, in lieu of green with scarlet facings.

1867

June 6

The regiment assembled for twenty-seven days' training, and encamped on the Racecourse, Ayr.

July 1

Inspected by Colonel Pipon, Inspector-General of Militia.

War Office, October 16

Regiment to be raised to full quota, viz. 37 sergeants, 10 drummers, 30 corporals, and 837 privates.

1868

August 4

New colours were presented to the regiment by the Marchioness of Ailsa.

July 13

The regiment assembled for twenty-seven days' training, and encamped on the Racecourse, Ayr.

August 7

Inspected by Colonel Roche, Inspector of Reserve Forces.

1869

July 5

The regiment assembled for twenty-seven days' training, and encamped on the Racecourse, Ayr, under command of Major McAlester.

July 26

Brigaded.

July 28

Inspected by Colonel Roche, Inspector of Reserve Forces.

1870

June 20

The recruits of the year, numbering 117, were encamped on the Racecourse of Ayr, for fourteen days' preliminary training, under the adjutant.

July 4

The regiment assembled for twenty-seven days' training, and encamped on the Racecourse, Ayr, Major McAlester commanding.

July 22

Brigaded with the Dumfries, etc., Militia, by Lieutenant-Colonel Bartley, 2nd/5th Fusiliers, commanding brigade.

July 26

Brigaded with Dumfries and Renfrew Regiments of Militia, and a detachment of 2nd/5th Fusiliers, by Major-General Rumley, commanding district North Britain.

July 29

Inspected by Colonel W. Gordon, C. B., A. A. G

1871

June 5

The recruits of the year, numbering 163, were encamped on the Racecourse of Ayr, for twenty-eight days' preliminary training, under the adjutant.

July 3

The regiment assembled for twenty-seven days' training, Major Lord Garlies commanding.

July 28

Inspected by Colonel Gordon, C. B., A. A. G.

1872

June 3

The recruits of the year, numbering 215, were encamped on the Racecourse, Ayr, for preliminary training under the adjutant.

July 1

The regiment assembled for twenty-seven days' training, Major Lord Garlies commanding.

July 25

Inspected by Colonel Gordon, C. B.,

A. A. G.

1873

June 16

The recruits of the year, numbering 130, were encamped on the Racecourse of Ayr, for twenty-eight days' preliminary training, under the adjutant.

July 14

The regiment assembled for twenty-seven days' training, Lieutenant-Colonel the Earl of Galloway commanding.

August 7

Inspected by Colonel McBean,

commanding 61st Sub-District.

1874

W. O. Circular, May 11 and May 21.

FIXED ESTABLISHMENT.

Lieutenant-Colonel.	Majors.	Captains.	Sub.	Surgeon.	Assistant-Surgeon.	Adjutant.	Quarter-Master.	Sergeant-Major.	Quarter-Master Sergeant.	Sergeants.	Drummers.	Sergeants.	Corporals.	Privates.	Total.
1	2	10	10	1	1	1	1	1	1	20	10	20	40	1000	1119

June 15

The recruits of the year, numbering 175, were encamped on the Racecourse of Ayr, for twenty-eight days' preliminary training, under the adjutant.

July 13

The regiment assembled for twenty-seven days' training, Lieutenant-Colonel the Earl of Galloway commanding.

August 6

Inspected by Colonel McBean, commanding 61st Sub-District.

1875

June 14

The recruits of the year, numbering 202, were encamped on the Racecourse of Ayr, for preliminary training, under the adjutant.

July 12

The regiment assembled for twenty-seven days' training.

1876

June 5

The recruits of the year, numbering 246, encamped on the Racecourse, Ayr, for twenty-eight days' preliminary drill, under the adjutant.

July 3

Regiment assembled for twenty-seven days' training, under command of Lieutenant-Colonel the Earl of Galloway, and proceeded by rail from Ayr to Greenock, and embarked on board H.M.S. "Crocodile," for conveyance to Portsmouth, to take part in the autumn manoeuvres.

July 7

Disembarked in Portsmouth, and

proceeded by rail to Holmwood, and joined Second Army Corps.

Encamped on Holmwood Common.

July 17

Inspected by H.R.H. the Field-Marshal Commanding-in-Chief.

July 18

Regiment proceeded by rail from Dorking to Guildford, and from thence marched to Aldershot.

July 19

Encamped on Cove Common, near Aldershot.

July 21

Inspected by Major-General

McMurdo, C. B., commanding 1st Brigade, Third Division Second Army Corps.

July 24

Proceeded by rail from Farnborough station to Portsmouth, and embarked on board H.M.S. "Crocodile," for conveyance to Greenock.

July 28

Disembarked at Greenock, proceeded by rail to Ayr, and dismissed from training.

1877
June 11

The recruits of the year, numbering

219, encamped on the Racecourse, Ayr, for twenty-eight days' preliminary drill under the adjutant.

July 9

The regiment assembled for twenty-seven days' training. Lieut.-Col. the Earl of Galloway commanding.

August 2

Inspected by Col. McBean, commanding 61st Sub-District.

1878

June 3

The recruits of the year, numbering 205, encamped on the Racecourse, Ayr, for twenty-eight days' preliminary training, under the adjutant.

July 1

    The regiment assembled for twenty-seven days' training.

July 25

    Inspected by Lieut.-General D. Stewart, commanding N. B. District.

July 27

    Dismissed from training.

1879

June 9

    The recruits of the year, numbering 189, encamped on the Racecourse, Ayr, for twenty-eight days' preliminary drill under the adjutant.

July 7

Regiment assembled for twenty days' training.

Lieut.-Col. the Earl of Galloway commanding.

July 24

Inspected by Major-General Bruce, commanding N. B. District.

1880

June 7

The recruits of the year, numbering 174, encamped on the Racecourse for twenty-eight days' preliminary drill, under the adjutant.

July 5

Regiment assembled for twenty-seven days' training.

Lieut.-Col. the Earl of Galloway commanding.

1881

June 5

The recruits of the year, numbering 151, encamped on the Racecourse for twenty-eight days' preliminary drill, under the adjutant.

The name of the regiment was this year changed from "The Prince Regent's Royal Ayr and Wigtown Milita," to "The 4th Battalion Royal Scots Fusiliers." The territorial regiment of which the Ayr Militia is the 4th Battalion is as follows:—

   1st Battalion (21st Foot).

   2nd Battalion (21st Foot).

   3rd Battalion (Scottish Borders Militia).

   4th Battalion (Royal Ayr and Wigtown Militia).

July 10

   Regiment assembled for twenty-seven days' training. Lieut.-Col. the Earl of Galloway commanding.

August 4

   Inspected by Colonel Herbert, commanding 21st Regimental District.

August 5

   Inspected by Major-General

McDonald, commanding N. B. District.

1882

July 11

Regiment assembled for twenty-seven days' training. Lieut.-Col. the Earl of Galloway commanding.

July 28

By an Order in Council on the 20th July 1882, the period of training and exercise of the battalion was extended to fifty-six days.

August 30

Inspected by Colonel Herbert, commanding 21st Regimental District.

August 31

Inspected by Colonel Herbert, commanding 21st Regimental District.

September

The old colours of the Kirkcudbright and Wigtown North British Militia, which had been for some time in the possession of Sir William Maxwell, Bart., of Cardoness, were presented by him to the officers of the 4th Battalion Royal Scots Fusiliers, and are now hung up in their mess-room during the training.

The regimental colour is yellow.

1883

July 9

The regiment assembled for training on Monday, 9th July. They were inspected by Major-General McDonald, commanding the forces in North Britain, and also by Colonel Allan, commanding 21st Regimental District, Ayr. The regiment was dismissed from training on Saturday, 4th August.

The old regimental colour which was in Dumbarton Castle has, on the wish being expressed by some of the officers, been returned to the regiment.

4TH BATTALION ROYAL SCOTS FUSILERS.

(Royal Ayr and Wigtown.)

Hon. Colonel.

Right Honourable Sir James Fergusson, Bart.

Lieut.-Col. Commandant.

Earl of Galloway, p.s.

Majors.

Sir William Cunninghame, Bart., V.C.

T. Riddell Carre, p.s.

Captains.

Charles Dalrymple, p.s.

Sir Herbert E. Maxwell, Bart., p.s.

W. H. Campbell, p.s.

James F. Dalrymple Hay, p.s.t.

J. M. Morton, p.s.

A. B. Gemmell, p.s.

C. G. Buchanan, p.s., I. Of M.

W. R. E. Dalrymple, p.s.t.

R. J. Bartholomew.

Honourable Hew H. Dalrymple, p.s.

Lieutenants.

J. McHaffie.

Q. G. Agnew.

J. M. Gordon.

F. W. Ross.

J. W. F. Hamilton.

G. J. Fergusson.

W. T. Cosham Hastings.

H. G. W. Gordon.

H. S. Sykes.

A. F. McAdam.

R. L. Nugent Dunbar.

R. B. Christie.

W. R. Birdwood, p.s.

Adjutant.

Major C. S. McAlester.

Quarter-Master.

W. J. Hancock.

SUCCESSION OF COLONELS, LIEUTENANT-COLONELS, AND MAJORS OF THE REGIMENT.

Colonels.

A. Lord Montgomerie.

Sir D. H. Blair, Bart.

William Kelso.

Earl of Eglinton.

Honble. Fred. Macadam Cathcart.

Sir James Fergusson, Bart.

Lieut.-Colonels.

Sir Hew Dalrymple Hamilton, Bart.

James Fergusson.

Sir D. H. Blair, Bart.

James H. Blair.

James G. Farquhar.

William Smith Neil.

Sir T. M. Cunninghame, Bart.

Sir James Fergusson, Bart.
Earl of Galloway.

Majors.

James Fergusson.
Sir. D. H. Blair, Bart.
James H. Blair.
James G. Farquhar.
John Chalmers.
William Smith Neil.
Thomas M. Cuninghame.
C. S. McAlester.
Walter Ferrier Hamilton.
Robert D. Fergusson.
William Charles S. Hamilton.
William Fred. B. G. Fergusson.
Lord Garlies.
William Cooper.
Sir W. M. Cuninghame, Bart., V. C.

Alexander McLachlan.

T. Riddell Carre.

Originally Printed by T. and A.
Constable, Printers to Her Majesty,
at the Edinburgh University Press.

2011 edition published by South
Ayrshire Libraries and printed by
LSI (UK), Milton Keynes.

www.ingramcontent.com/pod-product-compliance
Lightning Source LLC
Chambersburg PA
CBHW031406040426
42444CB00005B/443